Angels Come and Sleep With Me

A CHILDREN'S PRAYER

Text *by* Regina Cerda

Paintings *by* Jessel Miller

Angels Come and Sleep With Me
A Children's Prayer

Angels Come and Sleep With Me
A Children's Prayer

Text copyright © 1998 Regina Cerda
Illustrations copyright © 1998 Jessel Miller

Library of Congress Number: 98-93166

Publisher's Cataloging -in-Publication
(Provided by Quality Books, Inc.)

Cerda, Regina
    Angels come and sleep with me : a children's prayer /
text by Regina Cerda ; paintings by Jessel Miller. — 1st
ed.
    p. cm.
    SUMMARY: An illustrated bedtime prayer for little
children.
ISBN: 0-9665153-0-7

    1. Children—Prayer-books and devotions. 2. Angels-
Juvenile literature.   I. Miller, Jessel. II. Title

BV4870.C47 1998   242'.82
                                    QBI98-841

You may order additional copies of this book by writing:

Children's Prayer
P. O. Box 14
Deer Park, CA 94576

or visit us at our web site
WWW.GINADESIGNS.COM

Typography design and layout by Connie Burton
Printed by Tien Wah Press, Singapore

To

Déva and Lauren

and

All Children

Angels
come
and sleep
with me ~
each
and every
night.

Come
surround me
softly
with your
warm,
white
light.

Take away
the little fears
that
the day
may bring.

Let me
come and
fly
with you
out upon
your
wing.

If you and I
should choose
to be
the very best
of friends…

I will lead
a peaceful life.
Our love
will
never end.

This prayer came from deep within my heart
at the beginning of my
conscious journey
towards spirit.
When I wrote this prayer,
I knew it had to be in book form
on the laps of dads and moms
reading it aloud to their children.

Children will then learn this prayer which will help them
remember their connection with the divine spirit.

I truly believe that if we have prayers
to get us through the times of joy and sorrow,
we will be strengthened.
The earlier we can learn to pray,
the more peace we will have in our lives.
I am proud to be a part of this process.

~ Regina Cerda